Kindle Bestseller's Guide - Simple Strategy to Market, Rank, and Sell More eBooks on Amazon Kindle!

BY EUGENE WALKER

PUBLISHED BY:

EUGENE WALKER

I0463565

DISCLAIMER

The information contained within "Kindle Bestseller's Guide - Simple Strategy to Market, Rank, and Sell More eBooks on Amazon Kindle!" is based on the author's own experience and research. The sources used for the research are credible and authentic to the best of our knowledge.

In no event shall the author be liable for any direct, indirect, incidental, punitive, or consequential damages of any kind whatsoever with respect to the service or the materials and the products contained within.

Table of Contents

Introduction:

Hi!

This eBook is a collection of various methods to successfully publish and make profits from writing a book and selling it on Kindle.

There are various steps involved and for your convenience, they have been categorized into 4 Chapters with each chapter consisting of subtopics which would help you to gain a clear insight of the book and the methods through which you can finally achieve what you are looking for.

A. Monetize Your Book

    i.   Profits
    ii.   Positioning
    iii. Publishing
    iv. Product sales
    v.   List building
    vi. Corporate bulk Buy
    vii. The Sponsorship Model

B. Choosing your Niche
C. How to write your Book quickly
D. Promoting your Book in Amazon

A.   Monetize your Book

i.   Profits

Profits mean, the traditional way in which the authors get paid by the money generated by the sale of the books, royalties and other revenue generated solely after publication of the book.

Amazon agrees to pay up to 70% as royalty, which is huge when compared to normal publishing. But there is a condition for that. In order to achieve 70% as royalty, you will be charged from $2.99 to $9.99.

But that is not a problem, since the price of your book is between two price points to get maximum royalties on your book.

However you can price your book from as low as 99 cents to $200, but the problem in this pricing is that you won't be applicable to receive the 70% royalty but it comes down to 35% when priced out of the price bracket ($2.99 - $9.99) mentioned.

As your price goes up, your sales go down, they are absolutely inversely proportional. But you would be getting high royalty when each book gets sold. It is your decision to choose between Maximum Sales or Maximum Profits.

How to balance between Maximum Sales and Maximum Profits:

There's a technique in which one can achieve maximum profits and maximum sales at the same time. Here's an example to show you how this is done.

Typically with a new book, one should start off with the lowest price in the 70% price bracket i.e. $2.99. Keep the book with same price for a couple of weeks and note down the sales. Then increase the price gradually say $3.99 and keep it on sale for another couple of weeks.

Repeat this process till you notice that the sales are going down. Keep track of the sales and profits in a graph.

Though it takes around 2 months to have enough data to observe and analyze at which price, both the sales and royalties are at a maximum point, one gets a clear idea on pricing the book.

Some Fun Facts and Calculations:

An author, Amanda Hocking has sold a million and a half books since April 2010 and making $2.5 million in royalties. By January 2011, she was selling 100,000 books a month. Now, obviously Amanda is an exception.

What if you sold just 10 copies of your book each day at $9.99 a book at 70 percent royalty?

That gives you $70 a day or $2,129 a month.

Of course, you can publish as many books as you like. Even if you're doing this part time it's very realistic to be able to publish a single book in a month.

One reason to cherish is that, a Kindle book doesn't necessarily have to be a 200 page book.

As long as it has good content, it could be a short story, it could be a short how to book, it could be 30, 40, 50 pages long.

So, a book a month is a very realistic goal. After 10 months, you'll have 10 books. So, each book is selling 10 copies a day. That's 100 copies a day. Now, you're making $21,000 a month, which is a quarter of a million dollars a year.

Once you do a successful campaign, Amazon will take over and promote your book for you on the Amazon website. That is one of the reasons why publishing on Kindle is such an incredible opportunity because as long as you're producing, building content that people like, Amazon wants to see you succeed.

We'll discuss the part of Campaigning in the later part of our Book where we cover different topics like everything that you need to know to promote your books successfully, make lots of sales and get it to that critical point where Amazon will take over the marketing for you.

ii. Positioning

Imagine, how powerful it is if you can get our book to number one best seller status on Amazon. The moment people find out that you are a published author, people instantly see you as an expert on whatever topic that your book covers.

If you can get to Amazon's No 1 Best seller status, it's like adding rocket fuel to your profile and career. Moreover, getting to No 1 Best seller status on Amazon is a lot easy, because Amazon has so many categories.

What we're trying to achieve is to get your book to No. 1 for one or both of its chosen categories being strategic about it, following the steps taught here, it is much easier to get to No 1 Best seller status than you've ever imagined.

By being among the top sellers, there is a massive credibility that comes from being able to say "I am number one best-selling author on Amazon".

Let's analyze the situation where people treat you as an expert.

Basically, being an expert makes you an authority figure on whatever your book is and as an authority; people will listen to what you have to say.

Now, it means that if you are selling any kind of product or service, then you are seen as an expert authority and a professional. Being seen as an expert authority stops you and your product or service from being seen as a commodity.

In other words, being seen as an expert authority immediately makes you stand out from your competition. People would much rather buy from an expert than someone they have never heard of or from somebody that doesn't have that expert status and therefore is just seen as a commodity and here is the key - **They will be prepared to pay higher prices for your expertise.**

Additionally, being an expert authority will open lots of doors for you – Meeting other experts in your field, making business with people, and getting funding. It will all become easier. Trying to get media coverage, getting through to journalists, getting media coverage becomes so much easier, as an author of a best-selling book. Clients and customers will start to seek you out so; there are lots of great reasons for using your Kindle book to position yourself if you're selling any kind of product or service.

iii. Publishing

Kindle allows you to become a publisher of other people's work, not just your own and being a publisher gives you a tremendous leverage. It helps you make lot more money than writing it yourself.

There are two ways of doing this.

First is to hire people to write books for you. In other words, outsource the writing. This means you can have multiple books being produced at the same time and you can cut your workload back even more by hiring to proof read, to edit and format the books for you.

Figuratively, you will become a publisher rather than a writer. This is a powerful way to quickly build up a big portfolio of books, all of which are earning royalties.

The second of becoming a publisher on Kindle is to help other people get published in exchange for a fee or a royalty based commission, preferably both.

If you are going to help somebody get a book published in Kindle and then promote for them and start generating sales, you can charge them 20% or 30% of the royalty they make on that book. All the work you are doing to promote the book will help you get paid on a regular basis.

There are lots of people out there with content, many of them who either don't know how to get a book written and in Kindle in the first place or wouldn't know how to promote if they did. That is something that many of them would be very happy to pay you to do for them.

The best people whose writings can be published are those who already have big following whether it's on their blog, through their website, through a Facebook page or on Twitter.

It doesn't matter what the medium is, what matters is that they can reach a lot of people who are already interested in their work. Since they have many fans, followers, visitors, it's easy for them to rate the author as well.

As said, once you do all the necessary things, Amazon will take over and keep generating sales for them and for you.

iv. Product Sales (Direct Sales)

A good thing about a Kindle book is that you can include links which can be the products and services that either you sell or you are an affiliate for.

You can make recommendations in your Kindle book and send people to a website, where they can buy products or services that you've been talking about or recommending to them.

But this comes with a psychological limitation, if you put too many links, people tend to get upset and they might have bad reviews which will affect your book sales drastically.

Best way to achieve this is to use links sparingly and try to link them to the most relevant product/service that serves people. Link only to those products that you genuinely recommend for your readers.

v. List Building

As discussed earlier to link the audience to relevant products/services, a better way is to use links in your book to send the audience straight to a product, is to build a list.

The way to be really successful in building up a list is not try to sell somebody something straight away but to add great value to your list and build great rapport and connect the readers with the list. Thus they become mentally connected and they will be happy to look at and buy products that you recommend.

Procedure to be followed:-

- You have a "Call to Action" in your book that offers some kind of lead magnet or ethical bribe in exchange for your readers' beamer.
- Call to Action can appear multiple times in your book, but instead have it at the beginning of your book, where the maximum number of your readers are going to see it.
- The users email id is made known to you, where you need to build up a list, and then start sending valuable and free content to them to build a good relationship with them.

The sales will be much more effective when you've established a successful relationship with them.

vi. Corporate Bulk Buying

Here's an example of a woman who took advantage of selling her book to a corporate company in large amounts.

A friend of mine has just sold 1,000 copies of her coaching book to a large company who were going to give a copy out to each of their executives.

Now, this is great for her for a number of reasons Considering she made a $5 profit on each copy of her book, that's $5 times a thousand copies. Just straight away, a profit of $5,000 just on the sale of the books.

The other advantages are, it's great positioning and it's a tremendous endorsement that this company trusts her and respects her work enough to actually buy a copy for every one of their executives.

And then, of course, there's this potential for her to sell coaching services. If that company is looking for coaches for executives, she would be the first person to be acknowledged as every executive of the company holds her book.

A thing you can do to increase the perceived value and therefore, put a price that you can charge is to use Amazon's Create Space in order to do "Print On Demand" physical copies. Chapter 4 covers a lot more in Create Space.

But basically, Create Space is a company owned by Amazon that does print on demand physical books, unlike the old days, where getting your book printed meant that you have to put a minimum order of hundreds of copies and you have to spend thousands of dollars .

The technology has advanced and now you can get a single book done at a time.

A typical book around 150 to 200 pages, assuming to be in black and white with the exception of the cover, would cost you a $4 or $5 a copy.

And achieving Amazon No. 1 best seller status before you actually set the deal will make the whole process easier as Amazon tends to give their best sellers extra credibility.
An ideal strategic approach would be:

1. Publish a book on Kindle.
2. Promote it and get it to number one best seller status.
3. Approach the organization and convince them to buy your books.
4. Use Create Space to print physical copies of the book

vii.   Sponsorship Model

Sponsorship Model is a great way of selling hundreds and thousands of books at once, though the methods used are same as Corporate Bulk Buy.

While discussing Sponsorship Model, "Brendon Burchard" needs to be mentioned.

Brendon has had two New York Times number one best sellers and he had them within 18 months of each other, which is an incredible achievement.

Sponsorship Model works by finding a profit organization or a non-profit organization, whose members or supporters would benefit from getting a copy of the book.

The next step is to find a corporate sponsor who would like to reach them, generate goodwill as well as sending them a marketing piece of the book.

Then, brokering a deal in which you get a corporate sponsor to pay for your book to be given for free to that target audience. The sponsor should be given the book at a discounted rate. But this rate is inclusive of the margin on the book price for the author.

Thus everyone gets profited by such transaction.

Look at a quick calculation of how this method might work. Consider the sponsor buying 5,000 copies of your book whose cover price might be $15, but instead you provide the sponsor at $10 per book which cost you around $5 a copy. You make a profit of $5 a book times 5,000 which is $25,000 profit in a single deal.

Considering you charge an administration fee of 20%, which is another $5,000.

So, this gives you a total profit of $30,000 by setting up one single deal, which is why it is considered as a powerful method.

It also gets thousands of copies of your book into the market place which allows you to build a powerful relationship with both the non-profit organizations and with the sponsors which is a great way to open doors for your book.

Now, in reality, a book can be monetized in different ways, and of course, you can also monetize each book in multiple ways as well.

Serialization method for maximizing your profits

Serialization is a great way of generating extra revenue especially if you are focusing on profits, product sales or list building as the main way of monetizing your book which works for both Fiction and Non-Fiction books as well.

Serialization could be a series of books that follow on from one to another, such as Harry Potter where you've got seven books that together have sold 450 million copies.

Or it can be a trilogy, like 50 Shades of Grey in its two sequels which together have sold 60 million copies.

Generally a second book starts, where the first has left.

Another way that you can serialize you books is to have a character that appears in a series of books which has been a successful method in detective novels *like Sherlock Holmes or Hercule Poirot.*

Or it could be the formulae approach such as that taken by romance publisher, Mills and Boon. Here, the characters don't stay the same, the stories are different. But what keeps people coming back again and again is that they've got a successful formula.

The readers know what to expect and they like it. They keep coming back and buy more and more books.

In case of Non-Fiction, it could be a Training Guide or a 'How To' advice series, in which each book covers a distinct topic area.

For example, say you are writing about social media, that's a really big topic. Instead of writing one huge book, you could break that down and have one book on Facebook, one on Twitter, one on Pinterest, the other one on YouTube, etc. So, you end up with a whole series of books.

Or it can be about traveling and you write a really cloaking niche travel guide with different volume for different cities or different countries. It could also mean breaking a large book up to smaller parts and one of the great things about Kindle is you can sell books for very low prices and still make a low profit.

If you sell a book at a low price, people's expectations are different. If somebody buys a Kindle book for $2.99, they most likely aren't expecting a 200 page volume rather with well written and good content, they'll be happy with a short 30 to 50 page book or a report.

Even, selling it for as low as $2.99, will allow you to make $3.09 in royalties.

Now, to put it in a perspective, that is what a traditionally published author would get for a book that retails at about $20 to $25 mark in the general market.

And that's why the Serialization Method is such a powerful way of boosting your profits on Kindle.

Here is the Serialization in a nutshell:

◈ Sell the first book in your series at a low price to build a fan base.
◈ And then, sell subsequent books at a higher price. For example, 99 cents for your first book and then, $2.99 the rest of the books in your series. That way, you draw lots of people, get them hooked and then you make the real money on the second, the third, and the fourth book and so on.
◈ Always test the optimum price.
◈ Another great advantage of Serialization is that Amazon will cross promote your books when people buy them. It shows a set of related books, when people try to buy a particular book and the related books would be the list of the books in your series. What that means is you have three appetizing on the world's number one book site which will help you sell thousands of books if you serialize it.

Choosing Your Niche

Often writers find themselves switching between the British pronunciation and American pronunciation in their writings. In this part, we will cover:

1. **Choosing between Fiction and Non-Fiction**
2. **Choosing a niche – British or American**

Choosing between Fiction and Non-Fiction:

The seven ways of "Monetizing Your Book" apply mainly to Non-Fiction but not for Fiction genre.

Positioning:
As in fiction, positioning can be used in non-fiction as well, not to sell products or services but to sell yourself to build your fame as an author. As a well-known author, it is easier to get media coverage.

Another option is to publish in fiction space either by outsourcing the books or taking work from other writers and promoting for them.

List Building:
List building may not exactly work as in Non-Fiction, but it can be used to build a fan base, so that every time they feel something new coming out from you, they tend to buy that book.

This can be achieved through sending emails to them, showing a sample of your upcoming book thus increasing the sales when the book is released

Product Sales:
Product sales will not work in Fiction though combined with List Building. Similarly Corporate Bulk Buy Model also does not work in Fiction.

Sponsorship Model:
Similarly like others, the Sponsorship Model is not a fit for Fictional Books.

Serialization:
As discussed, Serialization is a great way to boost sales which work for both fiction and non-fiction and probably better in non-fiction. So there is a slight advantage to write fiction.

One of the good things about a Kindle book is that you can put a great cliff-hanger at the end of your book with a link just of the next book in the series. As people want to know what happens next, they tend to buy the next book instantly. And that just is another sale. The process can be repeated as long as content in the writings is good.

Though Amazon doesn't publish detail figures of the breakdown of their Kindle book sales but the consensus is that fiction outsells non-fiction. But that really shouldn't matter because sales in both markets are absolutely huge. What's important is picking a good niche or genre within the market that you choose.

Go ahead and choose based on what you feel most comfortable with and what you most enjoy working on.

How to choose your Niche in Non-Fiction or Genre in Fiction:

There are lot of surveys and figures available online about which niches and genres of books sell best, some of these can be very misleading because a lot of them apply to physical books sales but people's buying habits differ on Kindle. Part of that is because when reading something on Kindle; nobody knows what one is buying. Also, the demographics of Kindle are slightly different from the general physical book buying public.

So, how to get an inspiration in making a decision?

Given that one is going to publish and sell books on Kindle, a great place to look at is Amazon's Top 100 list for Kindle.

There are two lists:

1. Top 100 Paid
2. Top 100 Free

Though misleading, giving the book away for free for a short period of time is a great way to start promotion campaign.

In the list consider:

1. What recurring things do you see?
2. What books are popular?
3. What books appeal you as the type that you would like to write?

If there is something that's highly popular but it's not something you would like to write yourself. Have a look at both lists and see what appeals to you as popular and something that you would like to write.

List of Niches and Genres that sell really well on Kindle:

i.   <u>Non-Fiction Niche</u>

Whatever niche is found in Amazon in non-fiction space are in fact sub-niches of one of the three mega-niches.

1. Money and Business
2. Health and Fitness

3. Dating and Relationships

◈ Money and Business

This is really a broad topic.

Starting a business, buying a business, running a business, marketing a business, managing a business, selling a business are some of them. There are lots of sub-categories of business books to cover. There are many different aspects of setting up and running a business.

One of the great things about business books is that someone who has invested huge amount of time and money in that business, is highly motivated to see it succeed and will happy to pay for an advice that might help . The same goes for someone who is desperate to start a business; either they want to get rich or to escape a job that they hate.

◈ Making Money

There are always plenty of people looking for ways to make more money and to do it faster and easier. Becoming rich and/or become financially free is a very seductive idea. It's never going to grow old. This is especially in tough economic times, like, those that we're experiencing at the moment

◈ Investment

What do you do with your money once you've made it?

How do you keep it safe?

How do you make it grow?

How do you get enough money to gather for the kids' college fund or for retirement?

For a lot of people, this is really a big deal

◈ Self-help

Here are just a few examples:

Overcoming Fear

Increasing Confidence

Goal Setting

Achieving More

Time Management

Ending Procrastination

Better Communications

Career Development

Influence

Motivation

Relaxation

Overcoming Stress

There is huge potential for sales and lots of highly motivated buyers for Self Help Books.

◈ Dating

Anyone who wants to get into a relationship can't get into a relationship until they've got the dating things worked out.

The need to get that right is a powerful motivator that sells lots of books

Examples of topics might include things like:

How to get a date in the first place?

How to have a successful date once you've got one?

How to move from dating into a relationship?

Dating books can be aimed at men or women. They can be aimed at people in their 20s, people in their 30s. They can be aimed at divorcees who are trying to get back into the dating market. There's plenty of scope for serialization in the dating space

◈ Relationships

This can be anything like:

How to have a great relationship

How to save a failing one

How to escape a bad one

Having a great relationship in bed is another popular niche

◈ Marriage

Obviously, Marriage is effectively is a sub-category of Relationships. So, the same things could be covered here and to which you could add dealing with and managing divorce.

◈ Religion and Spirituality

There are highly motivated buyers out there for major religion or spiritual philosophy to write about

◈ Health

This is obviously part of the Health and Fitness mega-niche. Health is a huge in its own right. The list of health related topics is almost endless.

◈ Fitness

Fitness is the other half of the Health and Fitness mega-niche. Again, it's huge in its own right with countless different approaches to keeping fit appealing to all different ages, sexes, and demographics where there are new approaches being invented all the time.

◈ Weight Loss

This is a monster sub-niche of the Health and Fitness mega-niche. As more and more people   in the world become overweight, obese and diabetic. This a niche which is going to grow and grow

◈ Nutrition

Some people read about nutrition because they need help with their food habits particular allergy or particular illness. Others study nutrition because they're fanatical about their health. But in either case, both types are highly motivated buyers. This is a great area for niching down into very specific topics which can get cross.

These are 12 important niches within the non-fiction space all of which sell really well on Kindle. If any of those appeals to you, then there's massive potential and one would be very, very successful writing about something in that niche.

ii. Fiction Genres

◈ **Romance**

Romance is, always has been and always will be a huge seller. You will see the loads of romance novels in the Top 100 list.

◈ **Erotica**

We have already talked about how the "50 Shades of Grey", which started as an online, book that sold over 60 million copies. This is the genre that has exploded in popularity in the last couple of years.

◈ **Mystery and Thriller**

this is another huge selling genre and perennial favourites. Think of authors, like John Gresham and Dan Brown.

◈ **Fantasy**

Here you get to write about wizards, dragons, knights and fair maidens or whatever fantasy world your mind can ponder.

Some of the fantasy book series that have done fairly well in sales are Lord of the Rings, Harry Potter and Game of Thrones.

◆ **Young Adult**

And this is fiction that might appeal to older teenagers, all the way up to those who are in their early 20s depending on the book. The key difference with the Young Adult literature is that the protagonist will be somebody who is at the same age as the targeted readership and will likely be dealing with, sort of, stage of life issues that the readership is familiar with.

◆ **Horror**

Paranormal, vampire, zombies, ghosts, psychos and serial killers. Author Stephen King has published over 50 novels that could gather or sold over 350 million copies. Combining can also do fantastically well by combining two or more of these popular fiction genres.

◆

For example, the incredibly successful Twilight series is described in Wikipedia as vampire themed, fantasy, romance, young adult fiction where four genres rolled into one which seems to have worked pretty well with the series selling over 160 million books worldwide.

These ideas for both the fiction and non-fiction are just a starting point to understand what's right for you. It's not an exhaustive list but they're all good, either niches or genres that do very, very well on Kindle.

After choosing, don't get too hung up on the choice because you could always change it later if it's not working out or if you've just decided, prefer to be writing or publishing about something else. The important thing is to pick one and get started.

When it comes to getting started especially with writing, many people turn this into a much bigger deal than it should be, they start worrying about trying to get things perfect first time
And if that sounds at all familiar, you need to know something - Things are never perfect.

If you wait for a perfect time and you wait for the perfect idea, you'll end up never getting started. That can be really difficult especially if you're a bit of a perfectionist.

The best advice is to pick a niche or a genre that appeals to you. Spend a little bit of time researching it, come up with an idea and then get to work.

Other consideration, as you write that first book, your second book will be way easier.

It will probably get written a lot faster and it will likely be a better book.

Once you get going, it's easy!

Much easier than you think to build a portfolio of books.
All of which make Royalties.

A bowl which is generating income for you.

It is much easier than you think.

Just take that the first step.

1. **Points to remember:**
   1. when it comes to choosing between fiction and non-fiction, it really doesn't matter   which market you choose. Both markets are huge.
   2. Certain Niches or Genres consistently sell better than others on Kindle.   .
   3. Not to get too hung up on exactly what you want to write about.

How to write your book quickly?

Introduction:

The best practice to write quickly is setting up block time to complete a book. Setting up of block time is to set time in advance to work uninterrupted on a particular activity or project. Mihaly

Csikszentmihalyi, a renowned psychologist states that this block time is time which allows writer to get into "state of flow". This is also called as being "in zone" where the person's state of concentration is completely absorbed in the activity.

It is a fact that distractions decrease focus and productivity. It takes up to 20 minutes to regain full focus depending on the nature and extent of distraction. Distraction is stealing of time, productivity and hence earning power which is a tangible result. Block time prevents these distractions and improves productivity. There are three key steps to create block time;

1. Choosing a time
2. Managing your environment
3. Managing people

First, is to choose a time for block session which is ideally same time slot every day. Block time can be any time during day which fits into ones schedule.

A consistent time will help in getting into routine. Multiple block sessions in a day can be scheduled according to ones necessity to improve productivity.

Second, focus on managing environment which firstly means eliminating distractions like switching off mobile phone, landline or any social networking sites or messaging services. Secondly it means having all necessities for writing to be organized and ready for use. Lastly, the physical comfort of the writer improves productivity which means right meal and comfortable sitting position.

Third, is managing people to prevent them from interrupting the block time through training. Training of employees to understand the importance of block time and its role in productivity is necessary. It is much easier to get productivity through consistent routine and also allows employees to adjust to the schedule.

It is necessary to have scheduled block time for five or six days a week and one day off to rejuvenate. Scheduling the block time and recharge time will result in phenomenal improvement of productivity.

Steps to write book quickly:

The 16 step guide to write books quickly is a tool box which serves the purpose and is divided into two parts, namely Researching the book and Writing the book. Researching the book consists of seven steps and the later consists of nine steps.

Several tools from the tool box can be used but not necessarily all are required to complete a book. The tools should be used based on the nature of book.

I. Researching the book:

1. **Read three to five best-selling books:** Reading approximately 3 to 5 books will help avoid the law of diminishing returns. According to Pareto's principle of 80:20, 20 percent efforts will give 80 percent results. It means that when generating books on chosen subject, reading 3 to 5 good books on subject will give more result than reading 10 books. Using judgment in choosing bestselling books is key to understand the subject.

2. **Looking at contents of a range of books and observe the common themes:** Although reading 3 to 5 bestselling books gives good result it is also recommended to 'look inside' the contents and themes in books. This helps is including themes that might have been missed and allows for more research. For example the 'Look Inside' feature on Amazon helps in understanding what other authors have highlighted as important like chapter summaries, sections or action lists in a book.

3. **Reviewing top blogs and advising websites on your subject:** Websites and blogs can be reviewed using 80:20 principles as there is no exact number of how many should be reviewed. Top 5 websites can be used for reviewing authors' advices.

4. **Surveying customers and browsing forums:** Customer survey for existing and prospective customers is to be done for two key questions:
   - What is the customer's number one question about the subject?
   - What is the customer's major problem about the subject?

Solving these problems by answering customer's questions helps resonate with target market. This helps in gathering material for book and also what the customer exactly wants.

Interviewing experts: There are two reasons why author needs to interview the experts. First being that to gather research for book and second is that it is a way of writing book. This results in a book with collection of experts' interviews.

This step should be chosen after carrying out one to four steps for asking better questions. It is suggested that the author reads books written by the experts on chosen subject. If interviewing experts is a way of writing book then it is necessary to read first five to ten chapters with one expert per chapter to get their view at the outset. It is important to make clear the intentions behind the interview before recording and transcribing the interview.

The transcripts are then to be edited and approved by the experts for their inputs and approval for inclusion into final book.

Setting up of FAQs and SAQs: Mike Koenig's idea of gathering FAQs and SAQs brilliantly helps author in gathering information. FAQs are frequently asked questions and SAQs are should ask questions. SAQs are the questions which people should ask as they might not know enough about the subject.

The top ten FAQs and SAQs are to be structured by the author and used as a survey as in step four. These questions and answers for the knowledge of people might as well form the structure for the entire book and position the author as an expert.

5. **Searching on Google to fill gaps:** This step is about taking action in order start writing the book with 80 percent knowledge gained on the subject as it is hard to know everything about the subject. Googling the subject when gaps arise usually gives answers and helps continue with writing.

II. Writing the book:

1. **Brainstorming for ideas to get research on paper:** Putting all ideas from research on paper without holding back is the key to brainstorming.

2. **Highlighting key ideas and themes:** Reviewing all ideas from brainstorm session helps in highlighting key ideas and themes that stand out.

3. **Dividing the ideas:** Chunking ideas is a Neuro-Linguistic Programming concept which is all about finding ideas that relate closely to one another and then grouping them. The ideas related are separated into groups which further helps to work out the structure of book and review the best fit for final version.

Mind mapping: Either writing down on paper or using free software are options for mind mapping the ideas. Using software is much quicker and flexible to map out the main sections of book, the chapters and the sub sections within chapters.

Colour coding the chapters and sub sections is helpful for visual representation of the final fit of the book and editing to get a satisfactory outcome.

Starting book Writing: This is action stage where author starts writing book faster for quicker result using the structured research. The key here is not to stick or hang around a sentence, paragraph or sub section too long.

If a particular section is hard to complete, just marking it and moving on to further sections will prevent struggling. Probably answer can be found out when the hard section is written fresh after a break. To speed up things it's particularly good to take the help of a typist and have the book dictated.

This can be done either using transcription service or transcription software. Transcription service is old school where the author sends recorded notes and it is physically typed out. This is time consuming and expensive. Use of software is a lot cheaper in long run and is lot quicker.

4. **Using parentheses:** Using parentheses to indicate a particular tough passage or where there is need for more research helps move on and separate hang sessions. This separation helps review the tough sections and research necessary facts. It is more efficient if a separate block time is allotted for such sections.

5. **Reviewing:** The final book is to be left overnight and reviewed afresh after. This results in removal of obvious mistakes. Take help of others to review it to pick things that might have been missed. Giving deadlines to people improves the pace of reviewing and gets the work completed reasonably quickly as the book needs to be published.

6. **Final editing:** The final edit is done after incorporating the reviewers' comments and the final review.

Call to action: This step is necessary to include additional pages like introduction, resources guide and acknowledgements or copy right notice. Adding call to action is an essential way to monetize the book on Kindle if there is or is not a back end strategy.

At least, linking people to a page of book display and sale will help monetize the book. It is essential to put the CTA at the front of the book as most people see it. If there are more than one CTA, it is good to stick to one single CTA at a time to be tightly focused.

The most important CTA is to be at front page and have links to other books at the end of the book, especially if the book is a part of series. Additionally a review request at end of book on a separate page from other links is worth having.

How to outsource the book?

If one doesn't want to write the book, it can be outsourced. It gives a tremendous leverage if one wants to write multiple books at the same time by having multiple writers. There will be no question of stress but the downside is that paying for the work which ranges from few hundreds to few thousand dollars. The cost to outsource a book depends on many variables like:

- How long is the book?
- How complicated is the subject?
- How much knowledge does the writer already have?
- How much research writer has to do?
- What's the writer's experience?
- What is his/her resume?
- What country does he/she live in?

◆ What is the time scale for getting the book written?

The greater the cost, longer is the time to break even and make profit. If it is a short book for Kindle then it would take few hundred dollars. The person who writes for the author is often called as Ghost writer who can be someone with excellent English skills from college, or a person living overseas or someone looking for experience.

Finding a ghost writer is pretty easy as lot of websites do that, but finding a good and affordable writer is hard. There are many websites which provide platform for hiring ghost writers where the author simply needs to post a job.

The author needs to filter the candidates based on rating to create a shortlist of candidates with good rating. Shortlist the number to three after receiving test samples from the candidates. The three shortlisted candidates are to be sent same sample chapter for writing within a deadline to compare their work directly.

The good writer selected can be used in long run and will be worth spending a little extra. There are many websites where ghost writers can be hired like odesk.com, elance.com, association of ghostwriters.com, writeraccess.com and also by googling other websites or by using ghost writers' forums.

How to get a number one best seller?

Introduction

We are going to discuss how to get a number one best seller. We have a 30 step Promotion System to become a number one best seller.

The system is divided into three phases:

◆ Pre-Launch
◆ Launch
◆ Post-launch

1. Keyword research

Keyword research is essential whether the writing is fiction or non-fiction. Knowing the related keywords and phrases that people type into Google and Amazon is vitally important. Pick a best one among list of keywords researched.

That is how people will find the book when search on Amazon. The idea is to get the book found on Amazon and on Google. And because Amazon is such a high ranking website, there is a good chance that the book's Amazon page could also rank on Google.

Indexing on Google does depend a little bit on how competitive the keywords are. In order to generate extra sales it should be ranked high on Google. Type in all your keyword ideas. The next step is to take those keywords and test them on Amazon by typing them in the search bar at the top, the ones at the top is the most popular searches.

Amazon helps you know which keyword phrases are the best ones to use.

2. Choosing the Title

The primary purpose of title is to grab attention. The title should be appealing and mainly to grab attention. Secondly, it should be easy to read and remember. Next, it should create instant understanding. After getting a great title, sub-titles can be concentrated. Many things can be done with the help of sub titles.

3. Creating a Cover

The job of the cover is to sell the book. When a book appears in the search results on Amazon, it appears as a small thumbnail. Hence the title is so important to be attractive.

When the title of the book appears, it should be enlarged, bold lettering. It should probably be in all Uppercase and should definitely be in a highly contrasting color to the background, so that the readers can easily read it. A professional book cover can be done for as little as $5 in websites like fiverr.com

4. Jacket reviews via Author Central Account

It's a good way of helping to kick start your book on your very first launch with the help of the reviews. Before, it takes a long time to get actual customer reviews. Jacket reviews are going to be the same as the reviews that are seen on the back cover of a book in a bookshop.

Get some review quotes that can be added to the book's Amazon page. It can be done via the Editorial Review section of Author Central account. Author Central Account can be set up only after publishing the first one. It's free and you are allowed to add all sorts of additional material to the book's page.

5. Registration for the KDP account

KDP (Kindle Direct Publishing) allows the book to be published on Kindle. KDP account can be set up automatically with an Amazon account. A separate account is needed for trading through some sort of corporate vehicle.

6. Enrolling the book in KDP Select

KDP Select is a free service from Amazon which is going to be the heart of the initial promotion campaign. KDP Select is done on a "per book" basis and is done for 90 day blocks. It allows the author to give his/her book for free up to five days out of every 90 day block.

More the download and reviews a book gets, the more will it be noticed by Amazon. Until March 2012, Amazon counted a free download in exactly the same way as it would count the paid download. Unfortunately, they changed the algorithms and a free download counts for about one tenth of a paid download.

By giving the book for free for five days and setting the right promotion campaign up in advance, one can get thousands of people downloading the book. Amazon will count all of those downloads and this generates momentum when the book switches to paid at the end of the five days.

KDP Select allows people to borrow your book for free but still the author gets paid. Amazon has a monthly pool which it divides up based on the number of books borrowed that month. For example in October 2012, a $2.36 every time a book is borrowed.

7. Selection of Categories

When a book is published on Kindle, two categories can be chosen. For getting a book to that number one best seller status, those categories are vitally important. It's really important to avoid broad categories. If a too broad category is picked, the book could be competing against thousands of books.

That will make it very difficult for the book to get to number one best seller status. The more one can niche down to a small but relevant category the better and the smaller the category, the less competition the book has. More relevant the books, more responsive are the buyers.

This is how the number one status can be achieved. To find the right category for your book get into the Kindle bookstore and start searching through the different categories and sub-categories that might apply to the book.

And it shows in brackets, the number of books in each of those categories and sub-categories. You can choose categories that have a few hundred books or less than thousands of books.

The categories are very important because Amazon isn't like The New York Times that updates its best seller list once a week. Amazon updates its best seller list every few hours. So, when a book is launched, do the free five day give away.

Our aim is to generate as many downloads as you can in less time. In addition to this, when you switch to Paid, you want to get as many sales as you can in less time. Better targeted category makes it easier.

8. Writing Book's Description

People read the description when they go to the book's Amazon page. It can have up to 4,000 characters. Write something that is compelling, enticing, and also explains the content of your book. Give people enough information in the description to make a decision to buy the book.

Explain to them the importance of the book, its benefits and the pains that they get rid of. Include keywords in your description with a precaution of stuffing not too many. Stuffing too many keywords directly reflects on your writing and your chance of getting the sales.

9. Adding Amazon Keywords

For this a list of Top 7 and Top 15 keywords are to be chosen. With this Amazon will let you link up to seven keywords to your book, and can tell Amazon what your book is about. Make sure to use personalized top seven keywords.

10. Setting up Create Space account

Create Space is a company owned by Amazon and prints physical books on demand. By loading your book on Create Space, people have a choice of downloading the Kindle book or buying the physical book.

Most people opt for the Kindle version. A clever price can be done by having a physical alternative. If Kindle book is priced at $9.99, then price of the physical can be at $16.99. Normally people order the physical copy at $16.99. A higher price raises a perceived value of the Kindle version. It makes the Kindle version a better deal.

11. Getting pre-launch Amazon reviews

Get the pre-launch reviews before the five day free giveaway as they are great social proof. Try to get at least five, ideally ten four or five star reviews for your book before the launch. Honest reviews are very important, request for them.

Avoid fake ones. Many people can be approached to do a book review. You can either give them the book or you can get them to download at say, 99 cents. If one gets caught by Amazon posting fake reviews, the account could be shut down and won't be able to sell your book on Kindle ever again.

12. Sending hard copies of the Book to Journalists

This is an optional strategy. The question that they might ask themselves, is the book special in some way that might appeal to journalists? Is it ground breaking? Is it controversial?

Does it challenge the status quo? Does it have a great human interest angle? Is it highly topical? In other words, is it something that a journalist could build a good story around that?

If the answer to any of these questions is yes, then it's worth trying the strategy as it is not expensive. Use Create Space, to send a copy to journalists. Sometimes you won't get a response. If a journalist picks up a story for the book, it could be absolutely huge for your sales position and it is definitely worth trying.

When you send the book through Create Space, include a short note explaining why it is being sent. Keep it short because journalists are really busy people. After a few days, follow up by phone or email and find out if they feel it interesting to write about.

13. Setting up Squeeze page

This is another optional step. When a book is promoted online, there is a choice to send people directly to your book's Amazon page or can send them to a squeeze page for capturing their email first.

Get them from your squeeze page across to Amazon to buy your book. Use that email to build a relationship with that person and market to them. You can have a squeeze page that doesn't really capture email.

They can straight go from your squeeze page to your Amazon book page. But you can actually use the squeeze page to pre-sell your book as you're very restricted on your Amazon page to include the stuff that you want to.

If it's your own page on your own website, you can have all the images, all the copy you want to pre-sell. Put videos on there and pre-sell the book, from there, you can send them to your Amazon page.

You offer them some ethical bribe like free report, or access to a video or some kind of bonus that makes it worthwhile for them to give you their email in return for the purchase of your book. The next step is to ask them to go to Amazon and buy your book and give them a big button to click on that to open your book's Amazon page in a new window.

Also tell them to come back to this page to enter their first name, email and Amazon order number in the relevant fields after purchasing the book. And underneath that, you should have a "Get Instant Access" button they should click to receive their gift.

14. Listing Promotional partners

This step is the heart of the campaign. This is where you leverage the fact that you can give your book for free to get lots of people downloading your book and leaving reviews. This gives momentum to the campaign when you switch from Free to Paid, which applies to both fiction and non-fiction.

Find the top few in your niche or genre of the following:

Blogs

Advice websites

Forums

Facebook, people, pages or groups

And Twitter personalities

And what you're looking for is a list of the top five or ten of each in your space. Because there's going to be lot more than five or ten.

And if not careful, one has to spend too much time on this step. By applying the 80:20 principle get the top few of each that are going to give you the most leverage.

Once you're done, you approach them with a killer offer by giving them high quality and highly relevant content that they can give away for free to their fans and their followers.

It's important to explain them why you're doing this. Make sure that they have a basic understanding of how getting lots of people download your book for free, gives you momentum when you switch from Free to Paid on Kindle.

15. Setting up Paid Advertising

This is another optional step. Set this up ready for when the book switches to Paid. It's important to say that the idea here is not to make money. This is a loss leader. The more people that you can get to buy in a short space of time, the more chance you have of ranking on the best seller list for your book's categories.

To achieve this concentrate your ads spread over short period of time and avoid Google Pay per Click as it'll be very expensive. One can opt for Facebook advertising or putting banner ads on relevant websites.

16. Finding free Kindle book sites to promote the Book

Searching in Google search for "free Kindle book sites", we get a number of promotional sites. Six of the top sites have been picked based on the amount of traffic they get. Use all these six and a few more as well, depending on the time available and again, set up this at least a week or some more time in advance of your free promotion.

17. Creating and Scheduling Press Releases

There are two reasons for this. The first one is to tell people about your book. This will only work if your press release actually gets picked up. The second reason is for SEO purposes, for Search Engine Optimization. This is to help your book's Amazon page get found on Google.

So, even if your press release doesn't get picked up, it's worth doing just for the SEO benefits. There are a couple of sites to do press releases. The first is Prweb.com and the second is Webwire.com

Prweb.com is an expensive site as wide distribution is possible with it. And you'll likely to get more of a SEO boost. One press release through PR web and one press release through Web wire that goes out on the first day of the book launch and have a couple more press releases that go out through Webwire.com on days three and five.

By this, you can get four press releases out and can keep the costs relatively low. This needs to be scheduled in advance because the press releases will have to be approved in advance before they can be disseminated.

18. Contacting Local media

Local newspapers need local interest stories to fill their pages. If your story is run by a local press, you'll get picked up more widely. Set this up in advance because journalists are busy persons. If possible, get the story to coincide with the day your book is actually launched. That takes us through all of the pre-launch steps.

19. Book Launch

It's time to actually launch your book. Does it matter which day to launch? The answer is yes. Sunday is the peak day where people search for free Kindle books. To get the maximum momentum, go in from free campaign into your Paid campaign.

See that your free campaign ends on Sunday. To do this start it on Wednesday. If you're launching your book from outside the US, it should be known that Amazon uses specific time, just be aware of that.

20. Emailing your List, if any

If you've got a list, email them on day one of your launch about your book. Ideally you should have a teaser campaign to tell about and to generate excitement. It's also a good idea to send them another email once the book is switched from Free to Paid, to let them know that they can get it for a price of either 99 cents or $2.99 for a limited time only.

21. Doing a follow up with Promotional Partners

These are the bloggers, the people with Facebook pages, and people with Twitter followers. Update them and encourage them to post updates out to their fans and their followers, to remind them to go and download the book. Send several updates over the course of the five days and let them know about any milestones. If your book breaks into the top 100 and becomes a best seller, make sure you tell them.

Give them a reason to post out. If you're involved in any forums and you posted a thread on the forum about your free book giveaway, stay engaged with them, answer questions. Keep that thread active to maximize the number of downloads.

22. Post-launch Steps

Here we look at our pricing strategy when switched from Free to Paid. When the book switches to Paid, keep the price relatively low. You can increase it later but right now, capitalize only on the momentum of your free launch.

The suggested price is 99 cents to $2.99; the same weighting has been given by Amazon to a book until spring of 2012, whether it's 99 cents or

$9.99. But that is now changed. So, start by pricing your book at $9.99. You should start at $2.99 because it's still low to below risk purchase. But you're going get a lot more weighting from Amazon.

It's going to take you from the 35 percent royalty bracket straight into the 70 percent royalty bracket. And just to repeat what, to get the most sales in the shortest possible time to maximize the chances of your book getting up in the best seller list for its catcher, which in turn is going to generate more sales.

The next step is to find the optimum price for your book. During the first month or two after you launch, Amazon will start promoting your book. It will climb up through the Kindle rankings and eventually it will stabilize.

Try to track the daily sales and watch for that point where your sales start to stabilize. After that, consider start testing for price. If you didn't go straight to $2.99 when you switched to Paid, it is the time to put the price up to $2.99.

The next step is to test all the way up to $9.99 to find the pricing sweet spots. You already started on $2.99 and know your sales at that point, put your price up to $3.99 and track the sales for the next two weeks.

Then, put it up to $4.99, track for the next two weeks and so on, all the way up to $9.99. And once you've done that, you will have a day that you need to work out which price points generate the most revenue.

If you have a good back end strategy, keep your prices low to maximize the number of people that will see your book. But you still want to test because you may find that you can increase your price up to a certain point before your sales start to drop.

23. Tagging your Book

One is allowed up to 15 but you can't add them until your book has been published. You'll remember from earlier on, to have a list of your top 7 keywords and your top 15 keywords. This is what the top 15 is for. You are going to add those 15 keywords as tags for your book. Tags are publicly available. They appear on your book's page and people can search using them.

The way it works is that the more people that give your book a particular tag, the higher it will rank for that tag and the nice thing about that is that they don't even have to buy the book.

24. Getting some post-launch Reviews

You should already have some reviews from your pre-launch. The best way to keep that momentum up is to have a review request Call to action in your book. The best place for that is at the end of the book.

Have a page where you specifically request people to leave a review of your book. That's the point in time when they are most likely to do it.

25. Beginning paid advertising

If you are using this as part of your strategy start your campaigns for running the moment of your book when it switches from Free to Paid.

26. Taking Screen Shots

Your book will soon start to climb up the rankings for its categories. Once it gets to the top 100 into the best seller list, Amazon will start to show your rankings on your book's page and you need to be monitoring for this because Amazon updates its top 100 best seller list every few hours. You need to take the screen shots of your page.

However high your book gets, you've got a visual record of that. These screen shots are very powerful marketing tools and great credibility builders. Make sure you get them.

27. Updating the Book

Update your book and get Amazon to do an email broadcast to everybody who has bought your book or downloaded it for free. This is an optional step but it will boost engagement with your book. If you include a Call to Action, that will help with any back end monetization strategy that you have. This is how it works.

If you create a major update for your book, Amazon will email everybody that has a copy of it. You have to notify Amazon about the update. It takes about four weeks for them to review and decide if it's a major update and send out the email.

If they decided it's not a major update, it's just a minor change, then they'll make the update available to people through their Manage Your Kindle page on Amazon. An example of a major update might be something, like, adding a new chapter.

28. Search Engine Optimization for the Amazon page

Amazon is a high authority site; it's much easier to rank your book's Amazon page on Google than it would be to rank a page on your own blog or website. If you've sent out press releases as part of your launch, then you've already started the SEO process.

You can use Webwire.com now, which costs $25 per release to send out one or two press releases a month until your page begins to rank. Once it's ranked in, you can send out press releases less often. But still send them out occasionally, just to top up.

29. The 90 day Re-launch

This is another optional step. Remember the KDP Select allows you to sell your book for free for five days during each 90 day membership period. If you feel to boost sales, you need to run a similar campaign again.

There should be plenty of promotional partners that can be used. On the other hand, at this stage, you may want to move on to next step.

30. Going beyond Amazon

This is something that is important to know. You will automatically be re-enrolled by Amazon into the KDP Select program unless you opt out. The problem with that is, if your book is part of KDP Select, you're not allowed to promote your book in electronic anywhere else except for Amazon. If your book is doing well at Amazon at this stage, you may want to opt out of KDP select and start distributing it more widely.

Fortunately for this, we have Smashwords.com which is a great one stop ship which allows you to distribute your book through all the following channels:

Apple

Barnes & Nobles

Sony Reader

Kobo

Diesel

Baker & Taylor

So, by combining Smash words with Amazon, you've made your book available to all there is, the whole of the digital book market.

It looks like a lot of stuff but it really is easier than it looks and that is because it is a system. Just go through it in sequence one step at a time. Finish one step, that step is done, you can forget about it, move on to the next one and if you give yourself at least two weeks to get it set up, ideally a month, you will have a great success with this system.

And if you're going through the promotion, keep reminding yourself of the benefits. Lots of sales mean you're going to get lots of royalties and you're going to reach lots of people with your message.

Do the work of promoting your book once and you've got a recurring income because Amazon will continue to market the book for you and if you're selling any kind of product or service; Amazon number one best seller status is the ultimate positioning. So, that brings us to the end of our eBook.

ACCESS TO BONUS STEP-BY-STEP VIDEO TUTORIALS

First of all, we'd like to give you a **BIG HEARTY** Thank you for purchasing our book.

We strive to offer you the best service possible and certainly hope that we've been able to give you some kind of _**VALUE for your money's worth!**_

If you've learned anything or got at least **1 GOOD IDEA** from our book, we kindly ask that you share that with us and leave some feedback. Your humble feedback will not only help us to push forward with more helpful products to serve you better, but will also help other lovely customers (such as yourself) to make a purchasing decision as each review will be online for **ALL TO SEE!**

Once Again We Thank You for Your Time with Us and We Wish You **GREAT SUCCESS ON YOUR JOURNEY!**

(Just Click on the Link Below or Copy and Enter It in Your URL, then Copy and Paste the Password in the Box)

http://videoreviewteam.com/amazon-kindle-create-kindle-bestseller-6-simple-steps

Password: amazonkindle6

NOTE: Also If you want _**MORE IN DEPTH ADVANCED TRAINING**_ on _**How You Can Earn a 6 Figure Income Making Money on Amazon Kindle**_ (There is a Link at the Bottom of the Videos Page) ...**Thank You Once Again!**

www.ingramcontent.com/pod-product-compliance
Lightning Source LLC
Chambersburg PA
CBHW051249170526
45165CB00004B/1643